2017

Tarin Breuner

2017

Tarin Breuner

Print ISBN: 978-1-54392-309-4

eBook ISBN: 978-1-54392-310-0

To all those affected by the tragedies of this year.

Half of all author proceeds will be donated to disaster relief.

Porque mi libro está en inglés, escribo un poema especial para Puerto Rico en español. Ellos estan en mi corazón y merecen más pensamientos aquí porque son puertorriqueños pero también son Americanos. Quiero que los estadounidenses recuerden eso.

Un poema para Puerto Rico

Un evento horroroso

Una angustiosa pérdida de vida

Una destrucción de las casas de cientos de personas

Sin agua, sin energía, sin apoyo

Solo un desastre

Aislado del mundo

Pero con un espíritu muy especial

Más fuerte que la tormenta

Vemos ellos que se levantan del suelo

No solo con esperanza pero también con gratitud

Son con estos pensamientos que ellos siguen adelante

No solo para recuperarse o poder pasar a través

Pero para reconstruirse en un país mejor

No más visto como una isla rodeada por destrucción

Pero siempre una isla rodeado por amor

-Gracias y los queremos

2017

we will win it back with love

CONTENTS

Headlines, The Bad   1

Headlines, The Good   2

Game of Survival   3

Last Breath   4

The Next Generation   5

Perspective   6

Division   7

Women's March, January 21 2017   8

Executive Order 13769, January 27 2017   9

Land of the Free   10

We're All Pilgrims   11

Berkeley Riots, February - 2017   12

Wreckage of Hate   13

Fourth of July, 2017   14

First Responders   15

Charlottesville, August 12 2017   16

Bear Our Flags   17

Eclipse, August 21 2017   18

U.S. Hurricanes, 2017   19

Rubble   20

Hurricane Maria, Puerto Rico, 2017   21

Humanity is Kind   22

Las Vegas, October 1 2017   23

Everyday Heroes   24

Just Another Casualty   25

In the Wake   26

Voice of the Soul   27

Sexual Assault Cases, October - 2017   28

North Bay Fires, October 2017   29

Community Pride   30

NYC Car Attack, October 31 2017   31

Forever Raised   32

Sutherland Springs, November 5 2017   33

Remain Connected   34

Words of Thanks   35

Resist   36

Thanksgiving Day, November 23 2017   37

Southern California Fires, December 2017   38

Volunteers   39

Horse Deaths, Southern California Fires   40

Every Corner   41

Sirens   42

Remember   43

We Are   44

Live   45

2017   46

Countdown   47

Steadfast   48

Headlines, The Bad

"Killing Our Kids" New York Post, May 23, 2017

It's any other day

"Two of the deadliest mass shootings in U.S. history come just 35 days apart" CBS News, Nov. 7, 2017

It's any other day

"Amtrak Train Derails on Overpass in Washington State, Killing 3" NPR, Dec. 18, 2017

It's any other day

"'Dreamer' Plan That Aided 800,000 Immigrants Is Threatened" NY Times, Aug. 27, 2017

It's any other day

"White Supremacist Rally Triggers Violence in Charlottesville" Huffington Post, Aug. 12, 2017

It's any other day

"California Wildfires Now Deadliest in State's Recorded History" Huffington Post, Oct. 12, 2017

It's any other day

"Manhattan truck attack kills 8 in 'act of terror'" CNN, Nov. 6 ,2017

It's any other day

"Category 5 hurricanes have hit 6 land areas dead-on in 2017, more than ever before" Washington Post, Sept. 22, 2017

It's any other day

"Southern California's Thomas Fire now largest in state history" NBC News, Dec. 22, 2017

It's any other day

"In Puerto Rico, the Storm 'Destroyed Us'" NY Times, Sept. 21, 2017

It's any other day

"Hate in America: A list of racism, bigotry and abuse since the election" Slate, Aug. 14, 2017

It's any other day

Headlines, The Good

"One love Manchester" June 4, 2017

Love is stronger

"Country Rising" Nov. 12, 2017

Love is stronger

"Eagle Scout rushed to help, comfort victims of Washington Amtrak
crash" Seattle Times, Dec. 18, 2017

Love is stronger

"Defend DACA"

Love is stronger

"Charlottesville dedicates street to car attack victim" AP News, Dec.
20, 2017

Love is stronger

"Love is Thicker than Smoke" Nov. 4, 2017

Love is stronger

"NYC marathon runners stay the course, despite last week's terror
attack" CNN, Nov. 6, 2017

Love is stronger

"Hand in Hand" Sept. 12, 2017

Love is stronger

"Hundreds Helping to Save Horses in Southern California Fires" NBC San
Diego, Dec. 7, 2017

Love is stronger

"Somos Una Voz" Oct. 14, 2017

Love is stronger

"Our divided nation comes together to help in disaster" Dallas News,
Aug. 30, 2017

Love is stronger

Game of Survival

Walking down the street, killed

Shopping at the market, killed

Having a drink, killed

Watching a movie, killed

Going through the airport, killed

Eating dinner, killed

Driving through a town, killed

Studying in a library, killed

Watching a concert, killed

Going to school, killed

Leaving a concert, killed

Shopping with friends, killed

Riding a bike, killed

Watching a speaker, killed

Going to work, killed

Recovering in a hospital, killed

Checking into a hotel, killed

Trying to stop a fight, killed

Watching a game, killed

Going to church, killed

In a person's own home, killed

Living, killed

Life isn't supposed to be a game of survival

Last Breath

Can't watch the news without expecting your heart to ache
And yet people still dare to call these disasters "fake"
Until we are directly affected we turn a blind eye
It seems that every day there is more and more death
Each night thousands have taken their last breath
You don't want to use your last moments to cry
You cannot be human if you do not shudder
At the way we are choosing to kill each other
You have to share your love before people die
These innocent people have no reason to see it coming
And with our empathy we are never forthcoming
You never know if you will get to say good-bye

The Next Generation

With a world focused on the bad

It can be hard to see the good

Stop settling and you'll be glad

Choose change as you should

Take time to look and you'll find it

Tend to the heart before it's hurled

It will transpire if you refuse to quit

It is never too late to change the world

A promising future is never out of reach

To the next generation this lesson we teach

Perspective

Look for the good in the bad

Selfish – Self-loving

Impatient – Excited

Jealous – Adoring

Arrogant – Confident

Opinionated – Moral

Bossy – Leader

Nosy – Curious

Distracted – Creative

Moody – Emotive

Immature – Youthful

Regretful – Experienced

Careless – Daring

Indecisive – Thoughtful

Competitive - Driven

Turn words of hate to words of love

Division

An election like never before
Fighting back like never before
More hate than ever before
More fear than ever before
More division than ever before
Panicked reactions and protests everywhere
Tears and sickened stomachs
More division than ever before
One month and over a thousand acts of hate
Prejudice spiraling in all directions
More division than ever before
Raging anger on both sides of the coin
Bigotry in every place on every topic
More division than ever before
Words breaking into violence
Broken relationships and resting bitterness
More division than ever before
An America impossible to dictate
Nowhere to go in the wake of hate

Women's March, January 21 2017

A sea of pink
Notations of isonomy
A force of allegiance
Joining the fight for others
A feeling beyond description
Coming together with strangers
For equality, for acceptance, for compassion
Finding fellowship in adversity
Unity from uniqueness
Fighting for dissipating rights
Distinguishing the beauty in differences
All races, all genders, all sexualities, all faiths
No matter where they are from or where they are going
All backgrounds, all futures, all families, all careers
They discover home not in places but in people
Embracing personal identity in a world of billions
From every end of the earth, a common purpose
In a world so diverse we may only connect in love

Executive Order 13769, January 27 2017

A nation of immigrants

Banning those seeking a better life

Seven countries, 90 days

Families torn apart

Parents unrightfully separated from children

Slaves to the law

A nation of immigrants

Banning those seeking a better life

Seven countries, 90 days

Condemning the term immigrant

We are surrounded by them

So should we all leave?

A nation of immigrants

Banning those seeking a better life

Seven countries, 90 days

Either we're all welcome or less than 1% are

What are we afraid of?

Will we lose our nation to fear?

A nation of immigrants

Banning those seeking a better life

Seven countries, 90 days

Land of the Free

America
A new place
A place of dreams and aspirations
A place of great accomplishment
A place where anything can happen
A place where working and playing are equal
A place where kids are given childhood
A place where fun is a priority
A place of creating and inspiring
A place that strives for love not tolerance
A place of support and comradery
A place of sacrifice for a stranger
A place of hope for the unseen future
A place of unity and togetherness
A place of liberty for all
A golden place
America

We're All Pilgrims

The Mayflower landed on these shores in the pursuit of faith
Freedom of Religion is part of America's foundation
But there is a war against it all across the nation
Battling each other over what and who to worship
We shouldn't need to have so much grief
Surrounding a group's exercise of belief
Horrible hate crimes a regular occurrence
Do not let it be normal and pull down the blinds
We have to find a way to push the fear from our minds
Faith is the choice of the person and not the peers
The Pilgrims crossed the ocean to give us this right
Don't live in hiding and disregard their brave fight

Berkeley Riots, February - 2017

Opposing signs and cars set aflame
Abusive shouts heaved between sides
The flash and bang of a wielded grenade
Blazing declarations of war
The birthplace of the free speech movement
Torn apart by rival beliefs
Are we free if we are silenced?
If there is pain is it right to silence?
Words of love we always need
But hateful speech is never free

Wreckage of Hate

Life, liberty and happiness
Where did it go?
People are afraid to live their lives
People are afraid to do things they love
Where is our foundation? Where is our freedom?
A life of hiding is not a life
A true life is one of passion
A true life is one of joy
A true life is one of love
Look for the love
Look deep and look hard
Find the love in the wreckage of hate
Hold on to each other
Hold on to the hope
Life, liberty and happiness
We will find it again

Fourth of July, 2017

Fireworks decorate the heavens in bold expressions of light
A celebration of the winning fight for liberty
Elaborate parades and songs of freedom
Honoring those who offer their lives to the Nation
Flags not just raised but worn with pride
An unbeatable optimism for achieving the impossible
Endless opportunities to choose what is right
Stars and stripes enhancing every surface
Coming from all different places and finding each other at the top
Building a country from the grounds of Revolution
An infinite supply of hope and a matchless drive towards a dream

First Responders

Willingly putting themselves in the riskiest of situations
Not just for another but for all others
People they have never met or spoken to
People they know nothing about
People who they didn't know existed
Every single day for the safety of their fellow Americans
These are our heroes
It is not for themselves that people do this
And until they are in need, others are clueless
The fires, the smoke
The screaming and bleeding
The guns, the knives
The chasing and speeding
They would take a bullet for anyone anywhere
They need us to know that we really do care
They risk their lives every day
Cheating death with every action
Putting themselves in harm's way
We hope they get great satisfaction
They all deserve substantial appreciation
Each and every one of them in our nation

Charlottesville, August 12 2017

Hearts sank as the Nation seemed to step back in time
White supremacists brutally terrorize a town
Enlisting fear all around the country
Confederate flags waving and white shirts matching
Carried torches eerily reminiscent of the KKK
Public beatings over skin color, not stopped but videoed
Police rarely interfering as violence escalates
A car plowing into those brave enough to fight back
Young life lost, dozens injured and a broken city of thousands
Peacemakers arrested as igniters remain unpunished
America cannot give in to the racism
Those who do nothing participate in the hate
Those who live in fear give in to the intimidation
Those who stand against it are the ones that make the difference

Bear Our Flags

Malevolence is trying to tear us apart but love's bond is stronger

To fight back is to change the world

Pick up hope from the rubble

Stand for the principles of liberty

Remember what our country came from

We will bear our flags in this living hell

As Americans, we will drive forward, with more hope than ever before

Eclipse, August 21 2017

You feel as it begins
As it nears, the world is different
August becomes November
The wind howls with sweet sorrow
The air falls to a cool blanket
The animals are restless as the earth becomes still
The smallest sliver of neon under a darkening cloud of day
Like a mirage, it shifts and changes
It stutters beneath your eyes
Your vision turns to focus
The light stabilizes into a burning fire
A round of inferno in a devil's sky
Swirls of midnight engulfed into the dead of morning
A confused line of sight feels beyond what it sees
A divided nation finally looking at the same horizon
The ancients thought the world was ending
In modern times, it is a revival
The world is anew

U.S. Hurricanes, 2017

Harvey, Irma, Lee, Maria, Nate
More in between and more to go
Vision blurred from winds so harsh
A town that looks more like a marsh
Losing the line between land and sea
Devastation becomes hard to unsee
Terrified and scrambling for a way out
Never have we so wanted a drought
Thousands of animals left for dead
Watching helpless, our hearts all bled
Structures collapsing to the ground
Too many souls lost and never found
Displaced and lives falling apart
Cities upon cities forced to restart
Cling to one another in this disaster
We can only hope it will heal the pain faster

Rubble

They make their way towards the home that's no longer there

They trudge slowly through the debris and rubble

Pale skin and an aching body weary of exhaustion

They didn't have time to take anything but themselves

They ran for their life and left the rest of it behind

They look around at everything they have lost

A growing emptiness burrows inside them

They no longer feel sad, they merely feel nothing

They stare off not sure what to do next

They catch a blurry glimpse and rub their eyes afraid to believe it

Their heart bursts and tears of joy start streaming uncontrollably

Shaking hands and burning cheeks they rush forward in sudden urgency

They reach out to the pet they never thought would make it home

Hurricane Maria, Puerto Rico, 2017

An island swallowed in the devastation of tragedy

Millions without power, billions lost to damages

A fragile economy slaughtered in the surging of the storm

Crops destroyed, food gone and water unclean

The longest blackout in the history of the United States

Radars down and no way to predict the next storm

Injuries overcoming the lives of many

Hospitals without resources shutting down

A death toll that won't stop climbing

Neglected by their own government

They are forgotten in our hearts all too often

Not attached by land but in law and spirit

They have been left in the dark for too long

Humanity is Kind

Disaster strikes and we don't know why
People divide and look to the sky
But coming together is how we fly
So many didn't get a chance
In their memory we will hold our stance
Through this devastation we will learn to dance
And if we keep ourselves from going blind
In the future we are sure to find
That at the soul, humanity is kind

Las Vegas, October 1 2017

The sound of guitars

The rain of gunfire

The words "some days it's tough just getting up" sung into the crowd

The sardonic truth that, in that moment, the choice to get up was no
longer an option for hundreds of listeners

The spine-chilling switch from cheering and applause to blood-curdling
cries of pain and fear

The frenzied confusion

The paralyzing horror

Petrified and gasping for breath people cling to strangers as they press
their bodies to the cold ground

The bullets burrowing into flesh

The blood pouring onto concrete

Murderous terror collapsing a night of fun

The heinous desire to kill without cause

The choice to remove people from this earth by one's own hand

People celebrating love and unity blown apart

People dying over nothing more than where they happened to
be standing

Torturous moments of mayhem and panic closing the lives of people the
world didn't have a chance to know

A nightmare that will haunt those who lived and an early end for the
innocent souls who didn't

Everyday Heroes

The wild energy of people desperate to get out
The unfeigned sacrifice of those running back in
Holding together the broken bodies
Using oneself to shield others
Carrying strangers no matter how far
Not running from fear but running to help
Not thinking for the mind but doing for the heart
Blind to the consequence
Deaf to the probability
Risking the ultimate cost
The devotion to others is within them
And with a single action, the everyday person becomes a hero

Just Another Casualty

Why isn't it enough to hear what others had to go through?

Why does a person need to see it to feel sorrow in their heart?

Why is the reaction to doubt and let it pass?

Why is it so easy to hear of massacre?

When did a life become a number in a casualty count?

In the Wake

Hearts sink in the wake of disaster
Do not sink alone but rise together
Do not hide from the things and the people you love
Do not run from feelings in fear of them being taken from you
Do not feel guilt for the misfortune but feel grateful for the good fortune
Hearts sink in the wake of disaster
Reach out to loved ones so they know you are there
Ask people how they are so that they can see you care
Smile at a stranger in hope they will smile too
Thank the people who'll do anything to help you
Hearts sink in the wake of disaster
But hearts rise when they meet the hearts of others
Everywhere is somewhere, big or small
Everyone is someone, known or not
Every little thing you contribute matters
Every kind action benefits this earth
In the darkest of times of horror and destruction we find the greatest
light in one another
Let our hearts meet
Rise together in the times and light up the dark

Voice of the Soul

Music is the voice of the soul
Its melodies make the heart beat faster
It whistles the feelings we cannot show
It finds the words we cannot say
It's pure and relentless
It's daring and true
It lasts the years and bends the trends
It pushes us beyond our comforts
It teaches us to love and forgive ourselves
It teaches us to be open to the love of others
It helps us find truth in the dark
We find solace in the comradery of a familiar sound
A mutual connection under the song of a stranger
A soft end to each story
And after a year of catastrophe it becomes a platform for love
Performances for the masses
Bridging the gap of separation
Coming together for relief, for support, for bravery
Free fallin' into the arms of one another
Goosebumps from the solidarity
Living in the connection
Holding on to the love

Sexual Assault Cases, October - 2017

The numbers won't stop adding

Every news story is another name

Past and present

Person after person

Victims speaking

Cases growing

Bravery rising

Coming together

Voices hardening

Breaking out of fear

Standing against the odds

Believing in what can be, rather than what is

Time's Up for silence, time to change the world

North Bay Fires, October 2017

Blazing flames and skies of smoke
The narrow escape of a fiery death
The ash-filled lungs and gasping of breath
Heat rising with every moment
Air swallowed in a blue-less grey
An eerie loss of light and day
Innocents escaping with only their lives
With scary spaces and future unknown
Everyone desperate to find a safe zone
Communities gather together with love
The burning of homes a sickening sight
Hope-filled people refuse to lose their fight

Community Pride

Feelings coming out
Ribbons hanging from all levels of height
Old friends reuniting
Flags waving through the laden air
Neighbors holding hands
Letters of welcome at every entrance
Forgiving and honest
Signs of love and gratitude at every turn
Fortunate and smiling
Messages of hope, the language of the times
Uplifting realizations
A sense of pride in one's community and a reinstated belief in the world
around us

NYC Car Attack, October 31 2017

A chilling Halloween

A Manhattan bike path

Don't let fear run your life

Don't give in to their desire

A speeding truck

A deadly collision

Lives lost and bodies bloodied

Don't stop living

Don't stop fighting

A premeditated attack

An act of terror

Don't expect evil

Don't give up on peace

Forever Raised

A whipping banner of red white and blue

13 worshipping stripes

50 dreamlike stars

Forever raised

Through fire, through rain

Through wind, through pain

From the scathing mark of a bullet

Up from the cold ground we'll pull it

No matter the rage of hate

We'll always open our gate

Forever raised

50 dreamlike stars

13 worshipping stipes

A whipping banner of red white and blue

Sutherland Springs, November 5 2017

A town where everybody knows everybody
Families and friends gathered together
A room full of prayer and love
The entrance of a man dressed in all black
27 dead
A cruel act of murderous evil
Without cause, without reason
People punished for coming together
Love massacred with hate
27 dead

Remain Connected

Murderous acts a daily occurrence

Come together and end the recurrence

People tortured for entertainment

All this evil needs containment

Death keeping people from each other

Violent acts one after another

A person killed just for being alive

You have good luck if you survive

Pain should not be a rite of passage

The human being is not a savage

Too much pain by the hand of man

Stop the evil, believe we can

To any and all those affected

We must remain connected

Thoughts of support and recovery we will send

Look to the future and know this is not the end

Words of Thanks

Communities lining up to give officers hugs
Sentiments so sweet, they're usually on mugs
Grateful for every sacrifice made
Words of thanks, no longer frayed
Looking for ways to replace all that has been lost
But the things missed most are not those that cost

Resist

Evil doesn't drive us

Evil doesn't inspire us

Evil doesn't live with us

Love does

Create a new age, an age of love

In the face of hate, resist

The smallest action of love can overpower an army of hatred

Refuse to abide by its spite

Hate divides, love connects

Walk through the division and give in to the connection

There can never be too much love

Thanksgiving Day, November 23 2017

A look at the history of our Nation

A look at what was true then and remains true now

A day of reflection

A day of wisdom

A look at strangers and at companions

A look at the good in people

A day of community

A day of connection

A look at the beauty of the earth

A look at the joy of a simple life

A day of creation

A day of fulfillment

A look at the things we treasure most

A look at what we are so fortunate to have

A day of expression

A day of gratitude

A look at the things that bring smiles

A look at what we have to offer

A day of love

A day of thanks

Southern California Fires, December 2017

Living in the smoke

Eyes burning

Skies dark

A blanket of Ash

Watching the destruction

Homes lost

Tears shed

A blanket of Ash

Walking through fire

Neon flames

Molten hearts

A blanket of Ash

Volunteers

People flooding from all around

From every city and every town

Turning cars away for the donation box is full

Sending them to places of serious demand

Salvaging the last dollars for others and not ourselves

Letting time escape from our lives and extend to the greater good

Acting from empathy and not obligation

Choosing what feels right over what's convenient

Learning the difference between want and need

For a better future, we plant the seed

Horse Deaths, Southern California Fires

Ear-piercing squeals

Hooves pounding

Desperate cries

Gut-wrenching terror

Smoke-filled breaths

Hairs melting

Bodies scorching

Trapped behind bars

Fire creeping closer

Instincts not enough

Traumatic visuals

Loss of thought

Intolerable pain

Refusal to leave home

Burned alive

Every Corner

Love driven impulse
Booking the closest flight
Ignoring the money
Ignoring the miles
Trailers lined by the dozens
Rushing to aid
Rushing to give
From every corner of the country
Connecting in passion
Connecting in tragedy
Chancing the end for nothing or everything
Saving the lives of horses
Saving the hearts of people
Acting on love

Sirens

Sirens wailing, horns blaring
Lights flashing, yet no one's asking
It's become far too commonplace
Up and down like a ball, everyone ignores the call
We see the cars pass, officers rushing in a mass
Practically serve one another on a platter, like life and death don't
even matter
People take risks far too daring, others sit around not even caring
People are dying, no-one's crying
People should care before the end, people should care around
every bend
Every minute, every hour, every day, every year, remember to take note
of others, step away from the mirror
So then when the time does come
We will know each other, every one like a brother
We will love one another, each one like a mother
We will leave this earth, a lifetime after birth
We will think of in bliss, the people we will miss
And be grateful forever, for the love that won't sever

Remember

When you lose faith in humanity . . . .
Remember
Remember a time of community
Remember that person who gave you their seat
Remember watching someone helped across the street
Remember a time of leaders
Remember that soldier choosing to march towards war
Remember that first responder with sacrifice at their core
Remember a time of support
Remember the child who stood up to the bully
Remember the person who understands you fully
Remember a time of beginnings
Remember in these years our country is still young
Remember the drive that America is built from
Remember in little time how far we have come
Remember a time of growth
Remember what we thought was impossible then
Remember our pain, our mistakes and our past
Remember that as before, our tomorrow is vast
Remember a time of aspiration
Remember the issues for which people fight
Remember the next generation whose future is bright
Remember a time of return
Remember we are not defined in the moments
Remember we are how we react to the foments
Remember a time of love
Remember the dreams that drive us on
Remember the hope that brings the next dawn
Remember

We Are

We are lost in the moments
We are defined in the memories
We are lovers and fighters
We are dreamers and achievers
We are who we are
We are what we believe
We are our greatest desires and our greatest defeats
We are thoughts and emotions
We are actions and choices
We are shame and we are sorrow
We are laughter and we are love
We are intelligent minds and hopeful hearts
We are the light that shines in the dark
We are individual and we are free
Ultimately we are who we are meant to be

Live

May you leave this earth in peace
Live a life of happiness
Live a life of integrity
Live a life of adventure
Live a life of friendship
Live a life of forgiveness
Live a life of good health
Live a life of honesty
Live a life of confidence
Live a life of freedom
Live a life of compassion
Live a life of love
Live a life of gratitude
Live a life of dreams
Live a life of simple pleasures
Live a full life
May you leave this earth in peace

2017

With all the Nation watching
A silver ball suspended in the air
A year of tragedy suspended in the air
A year of division suspended in the air
A year of pain suspended in the air
A year of fighting suspended in the air
A year of disaster suspended in the air
A year of hate suspended in the air
A year of death suspended in the air
A year of destruction suspended in the air
A year of evil suspended in the air
A year of ends suspended in the air
With all the Nation watching
A silver ball falling through the air

Countdown

10

We will win it back with love

9

We will win it back with love

8

We will win it back with love

7

We will win it back with love

6

We will win it back with love

5

We will win it back with love

4

We will win it back with love

3

We will win it back with love

2

We will win it back with love

1

A New Year

Steadfast

Resist and overcome the pains that have passed
In our loyalty to each other we remain steadfast
Refuse to give up on the fight
Move towards a world shining with light
Believe in a dream, listen for the call
Believe in America, liberty for all
Drive to the future knowing you can
Believe there is good, not evil, in man
As the United States we are always connected
Hurt one of us and we are all affected
Join together hand in hand
Do not lose sight of our golden land
Through conflict we fought so that we may be free
And we will never stop fighting, even on one knee
We only get stronger as we are tested
So that we come out, chin high and broad chested
As we are hit, we will not falter or rattle
We understand there is no triumph without battle
At this look back of moments we wish to erase
Understand all that comes with your birthplace
Every moment of adversity takes us to where we are
Look to where you want to be, find your North Star
As your worries grow larger, your pain deepens and you fear
the unknown
Remember that we are in a place anyone would be lucky to call home
Built from hope and dreams since its very creation
America will remain strong no matter what hits its Nation